What Our Readers Have Said...

"Although I consider myself a seasoned sales professional, it is helpful to have past learning's refreshed. The books were also beneficial because of the information concerning 'trends' in the sales relationship. The sales process should be viewed as dynamic since business relationships change regularly."

•

"For the particular business I am in and the type of sales calls I have, I find that the books in the Pinpoint Sales Training Series are very often applicable to how I conduct business. I would recommend them to other sales people, just not ones that are in my industry."

•

"These books provide very good concepts. It fits in well with the Bell Leadership training program that I attended in November."

•

"I use this material in these books and apply it to my customers and other employees I work with."

•

"I would like to know other topics. Is there anything on Production Management or Consultative Selling or Time Management?"

•

"These books are great tools that should be used as guidelines for our everyday

supervisory practices. You need to take the time to do a short self-evaluation when reading them."

•

"The Pinpoint Training Series delivers information that could be used in a lot different areas."

•

"I like this because I can take them with me to read at a convenient time. I feel the little time I have to spend in the office is best use on activities that directly relate to revenue opportunities. I like the short amount of time it takes to keep up with these."

•

"I prefer the self-study approach; it fits in with my schedule."

•

"My thought is that the real value of these books comes into effect when doing the action plans."

•

"Short and sweet. These books are easy to comprehend."

•

"I have enjoyed reading these books. They are relevant to today's work environment and the ongoing change in the way we manage our workforce."

•

"I do feel that these books have been very helpful to me at my job."

•

"I think a lot of the recommendations in these books are very useful, and can be applicable to everyday situations. If nothing else, it's a good reference guide to fall back upon if a situation arises in the future."

•

"These books are relevant to today's work environment and the ongoing change in the way we manage our workforce."

•

Overcoming Price Objections

Pinpoint Sales Skill Development Training Series

TIMOTHY F. BEDNARZ

MAJORIUM
BUSINESS PRESS

Pinpoint Sales Skill Development Training Series
"Overcoming Price Objections"
Timothy F. Bednarz

Graphic design: Monika Pawlak

Majorium Business Press
2025 Main Street
Stevens Point, WI 54481
715.342.1018 • 800.654.4935

ISBN 978-1-882181-62-9

Printed in the United States of America

Introduction

The Pinpoint Sales Skill Development Training Series is designed for targeted training and education regarding increased improvement in a specific skill or competency.

Each book within this series is designed to be easy to use, understand and apply to your job. It can be used as a basis for training individuals, as a discussion guide or as a personal training tool.

Each chapter within this book discusses a specific concept. When you have completed all eight chapters you should have a 360° perspective of the topic.

Additionally, each chapter is divided into specific sections:

- The first section provides you with an overview of the topic
- The Implications section discusses why the concept is important, and why it is important to learn and apply.
- The Strategies, Tips & Techniques to Apply section teaches how to use and apply the particular concept to your work.
- The Points to Ponder section gives you something to think about or to be discussed with a group setting. These are questions not meant to be immediately answered, but to be pondered over time.
- The Training Activity section provides you with the tools to transfer what you have learned to your job. It is designed to help create an action plan to effectively apply the concept.

Each of the topics in this series is time-tested and proven in the marketplace. They have been used by thousands of employees as training tools. Many of the users have commented that what made these books valuable, was the ability to refer to them when a problem surfaced. They indicated that they remembered reading about the exact problem. They referred back to these books and found an appropriate solution.

You will find them equally valuable as a resource in your professional development library.

Table of Contents

LEARNING OBJECTIVES:

- To understand the causes behind price objections.
- To properly qualify a prospect.
- To educate the customer about the value of their offer.
- To use value analysis tools to demonstrate value.
- When to use price concessions.
- To determine when to walk away from a sale.

1

Why Price Objections Cause Salespeople the Most Problems

Customers telling salespeople their prices are too high is one of the most commonly experienced selling problems. The remnants of recessionary thinking dating back to the 90s, pricing issues have been compounded by vast waves of downsizing and consolidations and will continually remain in the forefront of sales problems.

Another pricing factor lies in the fact that the ever-increasing pace of technological change has produced a host of "me-too" products, relegating even more sophisticated products to commodity status.

IMPLICATIONS — WHAT THIS MEANS TO YOU

Now more than ever it's time for salespeople to ask themselves, "Why should anyone want to do business with me?" If quality, delivery, service and price are on a par with the competition, what will induce a prospect to select the salesperson's company over any number of others? Unless customers are given more compelling reasons to place the order, price will remain the sole criterion for their decision.

Many managers will suggest that price objections stem from poor selling techniques, and many salespeople do in fact use price as an excuse for a lack of performance. However, when a price objection is raised, it is an indication that something else has gone wrong.

Rather than caving in to customer demands for price concessions, salespeople need to take the time to probe for the real reasons behind a particular price objection.

STRATEGIES, TIPS & TECHNIQUES TO APPLY

Several areas must be examined when a price objection surfaces:

Price

Price may in fact be a legitimate factor. There is always a downward pressure to reduce costs—especially when the economy has slowed and companies are slashing their budgets.

In other cases, a specific price can simply be out of line with the competition. Since competitors are also under extreme pressure, many are given the flexibility to secure the customer's business at any or all costs.

Perception

Salespeople create perceptions of their company, products and services. This perception is supported by the image the company creates with their literature, facilities, products and other factors. When price and image are disconnected, a mixed and confusing message can be communicated in the marketplace. If a company has a high image and promotes a cheap price, the customer will automatically question the disparity.

Viewed as a Vendor

If the company is perceived as just one of many vendors from which to purchase products, the customer will view price as the primary factor. In their mind, the salesperson's company is only one of many choices. They have not been educated as to the value the company and its products are able to provide.

Insufficient Differentiation

Salespeople often fail to sufficiently differentiate their company from the competition in the specific areas that are most important to the customer. Once again, the customer has not been educated in the value of doing business with the salesperson and their company.

Out of Step with Customers

It's not what is sold that is important, but what the customer wants to buy. Many salespeople continue to sell products that no longer meet specific market needs, while acting like they are doing the customer a favor. Salespeople need to review their product line for products and services that are specifically attuned to their customer's particular needs.

Focus on the Sale

If a prospect senses the salesperson is only focused on making the sale, without regard to their needs and concerns, they will become defensive and resistant to manipulative selling techniques, which more likely than not will surface as a price objection.

Failure to Educate the Customer

Pricing problems may arise because salespeople fail to take the time and effort required to educate the customer. Unless customers understand the value they are receiving when they do business with the salesperson and their company, they will automatically default to the lowest price offered.

POINTS TO PONDER — SOMETHING TO THINK ABOUT

1. What is your typical reaction when faced with a price objection? Do you tend to cave in to price demands or do you probe for the reasons behind them?
2. After examining the issues listed above, do you see room for improving how you handle price objections? Explain.

TRAINING ACTIVITY — APPLICATION & ACTION PLAN

1. List the following topics on a sheet of paper:
    - Price
    - Perception
    - Viewed as a Vendor
    - Insufficient Differentiation
    - Out of Step with Customers
    - Focus on the Sale
    - Failure to Educate the Customer
2. Along the side, list as many customer situations as you can where price was a major issue or primary focus.
3. Identify the cause(s) of each pricing issue by indicating which of the seven topics listed apply.
4. When you have completed this exercise, identify any and all trends that have been indicated from your analysis.
5. Determine the actions you need to take to counter these negative trends and overcome pricing objections.

2

The Underlying Causes of Price Problems

The salesperson's failure to properly qualify their prospects is one of the main reasons potential buyers raise objections and are resistant to the sale. Without establishing a solid foundation upon which to build the sale, salespeople are undermining their own efforts. While they may think they are cutting unnecessary steps to make the sale, they are actually increasing the time, resources and frustration involved in closing it. In many cases they are putting the entire sale at risk.

IMPLICATIONS — WHAT THIS MEANS TO YOU

The price of a product or service is the easiest objection a prospect can make. Most prospects understand that a price objection immediately places the salesperson on the defensive. It's a way to back an aggressive salesperson off and deflect them away from the real reasons behind the objection. This buys the prospect time to make an informed decision, review additional information and data or mask their lack of buying authority.

Most salespeople immediately react to a price objection by reducing their prices. Salespeople must understand that objections are flags indicating the prospect has other unaddressed issues regarding the product or service. They must ascertain the specific reasons behind the resistance and any possible failures or missteps on their part that gave rise to the objection in the first place.

STRATEGIES, TIPS & TECHNIQUES TO APPLY

Objections typically occur for three primary reasons:

- The salesperson has failed to adequately educate the customer in the features and benefits of their products.
- The customer is seeking a better deal.
- The customer lacks buying authority.

A further examination of these reasons highlights specific situations in which objections occur:

- The customer has doubts and unanswered questions about the product, company or salesperson.
- The customer requires further clarification.
- The customer is seeking better terms and conditions.
- Salespeople may be rushing the sales process.

The reasons these objections occur need to be disclosed. Quite often the fault lies with the salesperson because they have failed to:

- Establish a need.
- Provide actual or perceived reasons for the prospect to buy from them.
- Determine if the prospect can afford the product.
- Determine whether funds have been allocated for the purchase.
- Determine if all levels of management have agreed to this purchase.
- Establish who has the buying authority.
- Provide solutions that meet the prospect's specific needs or expectations.

Salespeople must learn and apply specific vital sales skills including qualifying the prospect, probing for information, identifying needs and expectations and formulating sales solutions. They must also focus on acquiring critical product and customer knowledge, which takes time, research and preparation.

The second area of the salesperson's development concerns the acquisition of people skills. Salespeople must learn how to build rapport, credibility and trust with the customer. The development of a good customer relationship is the key to minimizing objections. If a strong rapport is established, the customer will be reluctant to raise price objections, or if they do this issue is generally disposed of with minimal effort.

The final area of the salesperson's development concerns personal motivation. Motivation impacts the following factors:

- Creativity
- Attitude
- Desire
- Persistence

The salesperson must be motivated to apply their imagination and creativity in developing sales solutions that specifically address the customer's needs, expectations and priorities.

They must also have a good attitude toward their profession and customers, the burning desire to succeed and the persistence to achieve their sales goals.

POINTS TO PONDER — SOMETHING TO THINK ABOUT

1. How often do you encounter price objections and problems?
2. What is your typical response when an issue associated with price arises?

TRAINING ACTIVITY — APPLICATION & ACTION PLAN

Since the inadequate qualifying of a new prospect is a primary cause of price objections, detail:

- The criteria you typically use to qualify a new customer.
- The criteria that will typically disqualify a new prospect.

3

Establishing the Product's True Value Eliminates Most Price Issues

Successful selling is creating urgency in the prospect's mind for a product or service. The greater the momentum generated early on in the buying process regarding the need for the product or service, the greater the probability the sale will be made.

The goal of the sales representative is to identify the prospect's degree of discontent with their current situation, then intensify that discontent with questions highlighting the urgency of making a change to the point where the prospect is motivated to buy.

The questions asked by the salesperson will increase the prospect's perception of value of the products they sell. An added benefit is that the asking of these questions will result in fewer objections. The bottom line is that an increased perception of value, linked with fewer objections, will most likely result in a sale.

IMPLICATIONS — WHAT THIS MEANS TO YOU

In the initial stages of the sales process, the salesperson should not be offering a solution or the precise cost of their solution, but exploring with the prospect how much *inaction* will cost their business.

Most problems and the complications associated with them have an associated financial cost. If the salesperson can identify these costs, they will be in a better position to justify the price of their solutions at a later date.

By giving the prospect a realistic appraisal of what they can expect to happen to their bottom line if they choose to do nothing at all, the stage for the sale is set. Once the salesperson has identified a real need or a genuine level of discontent, the prospect cannot responsibly afford to ignore the problem.

If the salesperson fails to educate the prospect in the value of their offering, they will fail to appreciate the financial benefits provided by the product and will raise price objections when it is presented as the solution.

STRATEGIES, TIPS & TECHNIQUES TO APPLY

Absent knowledge of the true dollars and cents cost of a problem, both parties will underestimate:

- The value of the solution being offered.
- The price of inaction.

When a unique sales solution is identified and provided to the prospect, the experienced representative will refer to the hidden costs of doing nothing and compare these to the cost of their solution. The point of emphasis is not on whether the prospect can afford the product or service, but whether they can afford *not* to purchase it. This is what creates urgency in the prospect's mind: an unresolved problem always costs their company money.

When salespeople conduct a cost analysis with their prospects, the following costs are identified:

- The amount of duplicated effort associated with the new product or service.
- The cost of extra supervision associated with a new product or service.
- The cost of training associated with a new product or service.
- The employee salaries and benefits associated with a new product or service.
- The cost of overtime.
- Hardware and software costs.

Next, the following items are cited in order to highlight the price of inaction:

- Lost time due to downtime of existing products or services.
- Money lost due to these periods of downtime.
- Total business lost due to downtime.
- Added costs of repairing and maintaining existing equipment.
- The overall impact of these problems on the prospect's business.

Invariably, when the costs associated with training and implementation of a new product are compared to the costs of not resolving the problem, the prospect will see a much lower purchase price. The salesperson has both created a sense of urgency to resolve the problem and presented a solution that will reduce their overall costs.

POINTS TO PONDER — SOMETHING TO THINK ABOUT

1. How do you create a sense of urgency in the prospect's mind? Explain.
2. What additional factors should be included to determine the true cost of your solution?

TRAINING ACTIVITY — APPLICATION & ACTION PLAN

1. Identify a major prospect or account you are currently working on. Use the following criteria to determine the true cost of your sales solution:
    - The amount of duplicated effort associated with a new product or service.
    - The cost of extra supervision associated with a new product or service.

- The cost of training associated with a new product or service.
- The employee salaries and benefits associated with a new product or service.
- The cost of overtime associated with a new product or service.
- The hardware and software costs associated with a new product or service.

versus

- Time lost due to downtime of existing products or services.
- Money lost due to these periods of downtime.
- The cost to repair and maintain existing equipment.
- The lost business due to downtime.
- The impact of these problems on the prospect's business.

2. Brainstorm and list any additional factors.

4

Utilizing Sales Expertise to Minimize Pricing Issues

If price were the only consideration in the sale of a product, companies would be utilizing cheaper and more efficient options for marketing their products and services than a sales force.

The physical sales call is the most expensive way for a company to generate revenue. The reason for a salesperson's existence is that price is not the only thing a buyer considers when they purchase a product. There are a number of other variables that necessitate and justify the higher expense of a sales force.

IMPLICATIONS — WHAT THIS MEANS TO YOU

Many salespeople feel that price is most often the major issue. If this were the case, they would be out of a job. There is a clear distinction to be made between price, cost and value. Buyers only focus on price when they have not been educated in the true costs of a product, which are often substantially lower than the price and value they will ultimately receive. This often occurs when salespeople themselves don't understand the difference and therefore are unable to communicate it clearly and concisely to prospects.

When salespeople understand the difference between the price, cost and value of the products they sell, they favorably position themselves to educate buyers in all of the critical information needed to make a qualified decision.

Without this essential knowledge, salespeople are only setting themselves up for repeated price objections.

STRATEGIES, TIPS & TECHNIQUES TO APPLY

Price objections are the most problematic objections salespeople encounter. Some of the common reactions salespeople have when encountering these objections include:

- Becoming upset.
- Agreeing that the price is out of line, then offering that they don't establish the price.
- Lecturing the buyer about the pitfalls of buying from the competition.

All of these responses are unproductive, undermine the sale, and send signals to the buyer that the salesperson will either give them price concessions or completely retreat from the sale.

Rather than reacting emotionally to a customer's price objection, there are several important points to consider.

Resistance Is Natural

The prospect has every right to be dealt with courteously and professionally when they have a price objection. It is unprofessional for a salesperson to complain or lecture about their price versus the competition.

The buyer may legitimately believe the price to be too high. They may have lower competitive quotes and perceive all offerings to be equal. They may also be testing the salesperson to see if they are getting the best price.

Whatever the reason, it is up to the sales representative to clearly demonstrate that their product is the best option for the buyer and is capable of delivering the best value.

Price Is Not the Only Factor

A prospect may express satisfaction with their existing vendor. However, if they were entirely happy, they would not be allowing alternative salespeople to make a competitive offer.

Undoubtedly, there are buyers who will base their decisions solely on price. However, astute buyers look at quality, dependability, customer service and a host of other factors that can be clearly delineated by salespeople to set themselves apart from the competition. These factors clearly convey a high value to the buyer that ultimately and realistically supersedes the price.

Value

The sales representative needs to use value analysis techniques that clearly demonstrate in financial terms the value the buyer will receive by using the product. The higher the value, the lower the cost. It is the sales representative's responsibility to identify the factors that deliver and establish value in order to dispel any unfavorable perceptions the buyer may have. This is how the salesperson demonstrates that their offering is the best option.

Avoid Competitive Comparisons

Salespeople weaken their own position when they introduce derogatory comments about the competition into discussions. They take the focus off of what they should be talking about in establishing that they alone have the best option available to the buyer: namely, the benefits and advantages they, their company and products and services can deliver.

POINTS TO PONDER — SOMETHING TO THINK ABOUT

1. What factors are important to your buyers other than price?
2. Beyond price, how can you demonstrate that you are the best option for your customers? Explain.

TRAINING ACTIVITY — APPLICATION & ACTION PLAN

1. On a sheet of paper, list all of your key products or services. Across the top of the page list Price, Cost, Value.
2. Determine the price, cost and value for each product or service in quantitative terms. This might take some time and analysis to identify.
3. Once completed, refer to these key numbers throughout your sales presentations.

5

Educating Buyers About the Value of the Offer

Most price objections and issues raised by customers and prospects stem from the fact that they don't understand the value of the product or service being sold. An insufficiently educated customer has only one criterion to judge and select a variety of products and services presented to them: price.

Unless a customer is educated in the critical factors needed to evaluate a product or service, many will not know what criteria to use in assessing the performance of one product or service over another. They may be distracted by misinformation provided by the competition or may simply not know what to look for.

All too often salespeople assume that customers already appreciate the value they can deliver or have the expertise to properly evaluate their product or service.

IMPLICATIONS — WHAT THIS MEANS TO YOU

Many salespeople assume their prospects and customers already know who they are and what they do. The reality is that salespeople possess knowledge and expertise that their customers expect them to apply to the sales process. This is specialized expertise that customers do not possess themselves. Additionally, prospects and customers often do not know who their salespeople are or what their products, services and company can do for them until the salesperson takes the time to educate them.

Salespeople can make their jobs easier and foster better relationships with their customers when they educate them before they even begin to sell. In so doing the customer will understand the way the salesperson works and what he or she requires to do the job properly. This establishes the foundation for long-term relationships characterized by shared respect and a mutual effort to attain a singular goal.

STRATEGIES, TIPS & TECHNIQUES TO APPLY

Educating a customer in the value a salesperson and their company will deliver involves imparting the following information:

The specific capabilities of the company and products that differentiate them from the competition

Salespeople must not assume that their customers know about the specific capabilities of their company. They must inform them of the specific ways their products clearly distinguish them from the competition. The greater the difference they can establish between their products and competitive offerings, the greater the probability of generating a sale.

The specific tasks or requirements involved to work on a project

Customers will typically be unaware of the specific tasks and requirements needed to successfully resolve their problems. Only when they understand what is involved will they appreciate the value of the service being delivered. Many salespeople work diligently behind the scenes without making the customer aware of what they are doing on their behalf. By keeping this to themselves, they diminish the value of the service that is being delivered.

The salesperson's qualifications and experience

The salesperson's experience and expertise is often the differentiating factor in many sales. While in the past it was the product that made the difference, today it's what the salesperson can bring to the customer that has real value.

What the salesperson can do for them

A salesperson's experience and expertise is of little value to a customer unless they can communicate how it will clearly benefit them.

The product's features and tangible/intangible benefits

Product features, while important, are not enough. Salespeople must also specifically quantify both the intangible and tangible benefits. Taken together, these three factors fully describe the capability of the product or service being offered.

A value analysis of the actual costs of using a product or service

Salespeople must fully quantify in writing a complete value analysis that educates the customer in the true costs of using their product or service, which when projected for long-term savings, renders the initial sales price far more palatable. This fail-safe method of closing a sale quantifies all factors for the customer to evaluate and provides them the information to make a rational and qualified decision. It is also a method most competitors do not take the time or effort to utilize.

POINTS TO PONDER — SOMETHING TO THINK ABOUT

1. Do you assume your customers already know who you are and what you can do for them?
2. Do you often assume your customers are aware of what your product or service can do for their business?

TRAINING ACTIVITY — APPLICATION & ACTION PLAN

While you may think you have this information readily available, take the time to develop a scenario that educates your customers about the value you can deliver to them including the following factors:

- The specific company and product capabilities that differentiate you from the competition.
- The specific tasks or requirements involved to work on a project.
- Your qualifications, experience and expertise.
- What you can do for the customer's business.
- The product's features, tangible and intangible benefits.
- A value analysis of the true costs of using your product or service.

6

Using Value Analysis to Your Best Advantage

No matter their complexity and sophistication, products and services are being relegated to a commodity status where price alone is the sole factor customers will evaluate in making a buying decision.

This is a situation over which salespeople have some control. Most salespeople find it easier to compete on price alone than to do the work required to demonstrate the value of the products and services they sell. Most fail to educate their customers in the value their products and services can deliver. Consequently, the majority of prospects and customers are unaware of how to evaluate the true value of a product.

IMPLICATIONS – WHAT THIS MEANS TO YOU

When a customer is asked to look at the costs associated with using a product, the salesperson is often able to convey superior value at the lowest cost.

Quite often competitors are selling products at similar price and quality levels. Most salespeople choose to meet the competition head-on in a battle where the best price wins. The astute salesperson reaches down into their sales bag for a valuable and effective tool—value analysis.

The use of value analysis enables a salesperson to introduce a higher quality and priced product that is completely different from the competition by clearly and definitively demonstrating its cost effectiveness and value. This strategy often clearly differentiates a product, proves its value in quantitative terms, and results in a sale.

STRATEGIES, TIPS & TECHNIQUES TO APPLY

Value analysis is the single most effective selling tool available to the salesperson. It is not a gimmick or fad, but a technique that has been successfully used for decades. It remains a stable and effective sales tool because it:

- Establishes the total costs associated with the use of a product.
- Quantifies the value the customer is receiving from the use of a product.
- Provides for the sale of a higher priced, top-of-the-line product with more features and benefits that drive overall costs down.

Effectively used, value analysis offers a distinct competitive edge. Most salespeople simply fail to utilize it. While it takes time and effort to perform, it greatly enhances the likelihood that the salesperson will land the sale. This is because many customers are accustomed to assessing a purchase from the perspective of price alone. They are asking themselves, "What is this going to cost me?"

When a salesperson directs the customer's attention to the real costs associated with the use of a product, they soon realize that the lowest price isn't necessarily the best value and option. Lower priced products and services often don't offer the features that actually reduce the costs associated with usage. When the extra costs associated with lower priced products are documented and compared to the value of a higher quality, higher priced product, the best choice becomes readily apparent to the customer. They realize that by spending a little extra up front they are often saving much more over the life of the product. Those savings can greatly offset the initial difference in price at the time of the purchase.

Effective value analysis should quantify not only the direct costs associated with the use of a product or service, but also the tangible and intangible financial benefits. The result should be a true representation of the financial value received by the customer when they use the product.

Any salesperson that wishes to sell value and build long-term customer relationships should remember the Sears slogan, "Quality is remembered long after price is forgotten." While some might consider this a ruse to trick the customer into buying a higher priced product, the salesperson that uses value analysis is actually performing a real service for his or her customers. It demonstrates how customers can reduce costs, increase their effectiveness and improve productivity.

POINTS TO PONDER — SOMETHING TO THINK ABOUT

1. When faced with price objections, have you ever quantified the costs to the customer to overcome these objections? Give an example.
2. Many customers look to lower their costs. Have you considered using this approach to meet this need?
3. Do you think customers would be resistant to this approach? Why?

TRAINING ACTIVITY — APPLICATION & ACTION PLAN

Examine one of the products that you sell and look beyond the price. For each product, document the following elements:

1. What factors define the value your product delivers?
2. How does the product reduce costs and increase efficiency?
3. What associated costs does your product reduce?
4. How can you place a value on and quantify these factors?

7

Price Objections May Not Always Be an Objection

The role of the salesperson is to *sell* value, not give it away. There is a generation of salespeople so indoctrinated in the philosophy that the customer is always right that they are not formally trained in how to hold the line on prices. At the first sign of price resistance, they are quick to drop the price to accommodate the customer. There is a fear that if they say no to the buyer, the sale will be lost.

IMPLICATIONS — WHAT THIS MEANS TO YOU

Price objections must be overcome without the salesperson giving an inch. Even the best customers will attempt to get more for a better price. But customers don't appreciate simply getting something for nothing. In fact, buyers are often afraid of getting something too cheaply. They want to believe they are buying products that deliver real value.

If salespeople invest the time and effort to clarify the value of the products they sell and educate their customers, it reduces the likelihood of true price objections. This also assures customers that they are receiving genuine value for the price they are paying.

STRATEGIES, TIPS & TECHNIQUES TO APPLY

At the first sign of price resistance, 95% of salespeople have the tendency to drop their price. However, research indicates that in most cases this is not necessary. Many buyers consider themselves to be adept negotiators. Price is often not the real motivating factor: they like to "be in the game" for its own sake, to negotiate a little and "win" once in a while during a price negotiation.

As price objections can be buying signals, the salesperson's first reaction should be to determine whether what they are getting from the buyer is a true objection. It may be a strong signal that the prospect is ready to buy. He or she may simply be trying to confirm that what has been offered is the best price. The buyer may be feeling the salesperson out for additional discounts or "extras" that may be available. The sentiment is that it never hurts to ask. Often the buyer actually gets more than he or she expects, only because the salesperson has failed to recognize that their objections are in fact buying signals.

As representatives of their company, salespeople should not be afraid to say "no" to the buyer. If they genuinely believe the price to be too high, the salesperson should look at the objection from their point of view. The buyer is often balancing the value of the product against the price. Consequently, many price objections are the result of the buyer's perception of the product's value.

While price is constant, salespeople can change the perception of value in the prospect's mind. To reduce the overall cost in the buyer's mind, the salesperson must establish and build up the value of the product they are selling. Salespeople accomplish this when they translate features and benefits into what they will actually do for the buyer. This includes solving their problems or fulfilling specific wants and needs.

Salespeople must focus on the intangible benefits the buyer will receive and quantify them in dollars and cents terms the buyer will understand. It is up to the salesperson to establish and reaffirm the value of their product and explain that it is properly priced, thereby establishing in the buyer's mind that he or she has already been offered the best possible deal.

POINTS TO PONDER — SOMETHING TO THINK ABOUT

1. Do you tend to surrender to initial price objections or do you attempt to determine the real reasons behind the objections? Explain.
2. What has been your experience with customers regarding price?

TRAINING ACTIVITY — APPLICATION & ACTION PLAN

Devise a sales strategy to change the buyer's perception of value.

1. Define what value means to the customer.
2. Determine what you have to offer that meets their definition of value.
3. Devise tactics and strategies that clearly and concisely communicate the value of your product(s) to the customer.
4. Identify ways to effectively communicate this message.

8

Should a Salesperson Make Price Concessions?

Sales negotiations are based on which party has leverage over the other. If the customer has a real need and cannot find a better offer, the advantage goes to the salesperson. If the salesperson is in the midst of a competitive situation in which the customer has multiple offers for what is perceived to be similar products, the customer has the advantage.

Many situations will be a "draw" in which neither party has the negotiating advantage. Here the customer may insist on price concessions and threaten to take their business elsewhere in an attempt to gain the upper hand.

IMPLICATIONS — WHAT THIS MEANS TO YOU

The key for a salesperson confronting demands for price concessions is to be aware of every competitive advantage they have. All too often salespeople will give up and move on to more lucrative situations. Yet in a contracting market resulting from recessionary economic conditions, it is simply too competitive to succumb to this attitude. When salespeople are that close to the sale, it is vital to persevere until they are able to close it.

It is essential for salespeople to appreciate that as more economic pressures are placed on customers, they must gain every possible advantage and concession they can before placing an order. However, this tendency need not translate into automatic price concessions on their part. Other concessions may include improved terms and conditions, expanded credit and other incentives a customer will perceive valuable. Such concessions generally don't carry a strong negative impact on the order's profitability.

STRATEGIES, TIPS & TECHNIQUES TO APPLY

It is a common fallacy to think that the customer is always demanding or expecting price concessions. While many would naturally like to achieve that end, they will often be just as happy with other lower-cost incentives to "sweeten the deal."

When encountering price objections salespeople should:

Verify the Information

The customer may very well be playing some games to get a better price before they commit to the sale. After all, they want the best deal possible. They may attempt to use the competition to leverage a better price.

To counter this situation, salespeople must apply their expertise and competitive knowledge in comparing features and benefits and educating the customer in the key differences between the two options. Salespeople should also obtain the competitor's price list—ideally from a friendly source—and compare who really has the best price.

Compare the Features and Benefits

In competitive situations, most products do in fact compare favorably with each other. With many providing similar features and benefits, the competitive edge will often hinge on minor differences. The key is to identify the features that are important to the customer, as one small item or difference in a product or service can result in the sale. Additionally, to increase product space and perceived value, salespeople must identify not only the tangible, but also the intangible features and benefits of their product.

Point to Special Terms and Discounts

It is important for salespeople to become well-versed in the terms and conditions they are authorized to make. They must apply creativity to "make the deal work" for their customer.

If all else fails, salespeople should enlist the assistance of their managers and senior executives to create additional incentives for the customer that induce them to place the order.

Look to Volume Discounts

Salespeople can seek to get their customers to agree to a long-term contract that ultimately takes advantage of volume discounts. If salespeople understand the product usage and buying patterns of their customers, they might be able to upgrade them to a volume that is more price competitive and advantageous to them.

Provide Feedback to Your Company

If another vendor really has the upper hand, salespeople need to provide feedback to their company concerning the competitive environment in which they are dealing. In a highly competitive situation and if the volume warrants, many companies are willing to meet or beat a competitive offer, especially during slow economic periods where every sales dollar counts.

POINTS TO PONDER — SOMETHING TO THINK ABOUT

1. What strategies do you employ to deal with demands for price concessions? Explain.
2. Think of the most difficult price objection you were able to overcome. What did you do and why did it work?

TRAINING ACTIVITY — APPLICATION & ACTION PLAN

Prepare yourself for competitive pricing situations by doing the following:

1. Become thoroughly familiar with the terms and conditions your company offers.
2. Review the product usage of all of your primary customers.
3. Determine whether they may qualify for better prices, terms and conditions if they upgrade to a long-term contract.
4. Compare your products with those of the competition and determine the key differences and advantages you offer.
5. Develop the competitive intelligence to identify the prices of each primary competitor.

About the Author

Timothy F. Bednarz, Ph.D. is CEO of the American Management Development Group, Inc. For over 20 years he has researched, designed and authored hundreds of learning and development programs used by Fortune 1000 companies.

He is also the author of *Great! What Makes Leaders Great. What They Did, How They Did It and What You Can Learn from It* (2011).

Speaking Availability

Timothy F. Bednarz, Ph.D. is available for speaking engagements for your next meeting or association event. He can be contacted at 800-654-4935 or by e-mail at timothy.bednarz@majorium.com.

Bulk Sales

Bulk sales of this book or any other titles available from Majorium Business Press. Inquiries can be directed to sales@majorium.com, or by phone at 800-6654-4935.

Quick Order Form

Fax orders: 715-342-1118. Send this form.

Telephone orders: Call 800-654-4935 toll-free. Have your credit card ready.

Email orders: sales@majorium.com

Postal orders: Majorium Business Press, 2025 Main Street, Stevens Point, WI 54481, USA.

Please send the following books:

____

____

____

____

Please send more FREE information on:

❑Catalog ❑Speaking/Seminars ❑Mailing Lists ❑Consulting

Name: ____

Address: ____

City: ____________________________ State: _____ Zip: __________

Telephone: ____

Email address: ____

Sales tax: Please add 5.5% for products shipped to Wisconsin addresses.

Shipping by air:

United States: $4.00 for first book and $2.00 for each additional product.

International: $9.00 for first book; $5.00 for each additional product (estimate).

Made in United States
Orlando, FL
16 June 2026

82935788R00026